CONVERSATIONS WITH MY GUARDIAN ANGEL

Sandy & Pat,
May Happiness be yours
for a very long time!

CONVERSATIONS WITH MY GUARDIAN ANGEL

By

Arthur Thomas Smith

AS TOLD TO

DR. A. THOMAS SMITH

and
Judy Strefling Smith

With Illustrations Inserted By

Micah Andrew Smith

May God bless you,

Arthur Smith

ISBN 1-58500-326-3

ABOUT THE BOOK

Throughout recorded history, angels have appeared and otherwise communicated with humans. However, the account which has been compiled in *CONVERSATIONS WITH MY GUARDIAN ANGEL* may well be the first record of an angel engaging in an interactive vision/dream with a trained student of theology who is a practicing psychologist..

While many books about angels are available, *CONVERSATIONS WITH MY GUARDIAN ANGEL,* is unique in that it not only presents an account of an angelic appearance, but it also summarizes Biblical references to angels, and answers questions about angels and their opinions which have gone unanswered for centuries. It is the intention of the authors that this book may be of interest to Christians and non-Christians alike.

Interactions with the guardian angel continue and it is also the intention of the authors to compile and then write about additional insights into angelic life.

TABLE OF CONTENTS

Title	Page

FORWARD

For centuries after centuries, men, women, and children have had many questions about the angels that God created before the beginning of earthly time. While guardian angels are with their human charges, they normally do their protecting without being seen, heard, or noticed. Sometimes, a guardian angel will appear through dreams, visions, and thoughts. They are visable with very rare exceptions only to their charges and likewise can only be heard by them.

This concise book is the result of a guardian angel visiting a human during periods of sleep and meditation. Under unique circumstances, the angel transmitted thoughts to the author in response to questions that were compiled by the author and his wife. While questions have been asked of angels before, this sustained interactive conversation continued for many hours and permitted the author to record the precise answers offered by the guardian angel.

As you read the contents of this book, keep in mind that guardian angels do not know everthing but it is their main goal to do everything possible to assist the human whom they are protecting.

My message which forms the forward of this book, was given to the guardian angel, who then provided it to the author.

It is our desire to further your understanding about the work of angels and also further the Kingdom of God by allowing people this unique opportunity to read about their spiritual guardians.

May God bless your understanding and provide you with inner peace all the days of your lives.

Archangel Michael

INTRODUCTION

January 1, 1998, and the events which occurred on that date and days following will forever affect the lives of my wife, Judy, my own, and members of our family. As incredible as the events were, time will tend to fade my memory of them and so I have prepared this written record.

After considerable discussion with my wife, we have decided to share these experiences with those who would like to read about them and perhaps learn from them.

From the outset, you must understand that I am by nature a very calm, good natured, caring individual. I am by training well read and highly educated in the areas of psychology, history, political science, and religion. My wife and I know each other very well having been married for thirty years. We have two sons, Shawn and Micah, and three grandchildren, Devin, Autum, and Seth. I am employed as a psychologist, and my wife writes a weekly recipe column for a regional newspaper. We are active in our community affairs and could be best described as stable good citizens who reflect the positive values of American society.

You must also understand that I am an individual who has very brief unremarkable dreams. For instance, I have had dreams in which I was eating a bowl of cereal for breakfast; in which I was giving a speech at a school faculty meeting; and in which I was standing on a beach looking at the waves on a lake. Perhaps one of my most memorable dreams was the time that I dreamed that I was having trouble moving my arms because the hair under my armpits had become tangled, and I was attempting to pull out the small knots in the hair.

That should give you a mental picture of what I am like and how we typically live. This was all changed on New Year's Day, 1998. We typically watch the Tournament of Roses Parade and a football game on a day like this, but it became very difficult to focus on these activities. During the early morning hours, I was sleeping well like I normally do, and having a dream that was completely abnormal for me. In my dream, I was standing, completely undressed and feeling ill-at-ease but not afraid, in a large room with white walls, ceiling, and floor. Directly in front of me was a white piece of furniture which resembled a judge's bench in a courtroom. On the bench was resting a white gavel. As I was standing and looking forward, a figure attired in a bright white, flowing gown, descended slowly from the ceiling. The figure seemed to be of average height for a male with lightly colored shoulder length hair, and fair facial features. It descended until it was standing behind the white bench. He looked at me for a few moments and then he began to speak. In firm, but kindly authoritarian voice, he said, "Arthur, you have been found guilty of committing several sins of omission." He then picked up the gavel, and rapped it once on the top of the bench. He continued to say, "As your guardian angel, I will carry out God's judgements upon you for committing these sins and then you will become pure in God's sight. You will also be called into His service." At this time, I asked my guardian angel if he could tell me exactly what these sins were. He responded that I would have to figure out what they were, be truly repentant for them, and promise to make changes in my life that would include no longer committing these sins. He bid me farewell and ascended through the ceiling. I felt myself leaving the room and woke up sometime later still feeling a rush of adrenalin in my body.

When my wife awoke, I got out of bed, walked around to her side, and said, "Mom, I have had a very unusual dream that was so real and vivid that it might have been a vision." I then explained to her what I had seen a few hours earlier. She was sort of half-asleep and also feeling somewhat depressed because our youngest son, who had been home on his winter break, was returning to college later that day. She listened to what I said, replied that we could talk about it later, and said she was not feeling well and wanted to return to sleep for awhile. She did that and I went to a local bakery to get some fresh pastries and bread items for breakfast.

When I returned home, I tried to watch the parade but my dream kept replaying in my mind. At midday, I helped our son pack his car, we jump started a dead battery, and saw our son off on his trip to college. I tried to relax and watch some television, but could not do it.

I began believing in guardian angels when I was a child and I have never abandoned that belief. However, I always thought that they were invisible protectors constantly watching over you. I had read stories about people who have seen angels and have also read Biblical accounts of angels and archangels, but had never considered the possibility that it might happen to me. During that afternoon, I was not ready to accept the idea that I had actually seen my guardian angel in a vision or dream but I could not keep from thinking about it. So, out of curiousity, I went downstairs to our home office/library where we have a collection of books on religious topics. I found a book about angels written by the Reverend Doctor Billy Graham. Keep in mind that I have believed in angels since I was a child with the understanding that your guardian angel exists to protect you especially in times of danger. The one thing that really bothered me about my dream/vision was that my angel was engaged in carrying out judgments. As I was reading Dr. Graham's book, I came across a paragraph in which he said that one of an angel's duties is to administer God's judgments while we are here on Earth. That really hit home and made me think that perhaps I had actually met my guardian angel in a dream/vision.

My wife and I discussed my dream/vision during the evening and had come to the conclusion that it was probably only a very vivid dream. That night, I took a bath like I normally do which means after washing my hair and scrubbing up I layed down in the warm water and went to sleep for about thirty minutes.

After my bath, and still half-asleep I gathered the laundry from the hamper and took it downstairs to our lower level laundry room for my wife to wash in the morning. As I was walking up the lower level stairs, I glanced upward and at the top of the stairs, my guardian angel was standing motioning for me to follow him. I felt myself going back to sleep as if in a mild trance. My guardian angel led me into our living room and he sat on the sofa while I sat in a chair facing him. We talked about what I had seen in the dream. As we were finishing our conversation, my wife called to me from the kitchen and he disappeared into the wall. I did not say anything about this visit until we were in our bedroom and then still quivering and with tears in my eyes, I explained to my wife what had just happened. We then concluded that I was having an interactive dream and the vision of my guardian angel was real.

In the coming days, we decided that if my guardian angel would re-appear, and if he would participate, I should ask him some questions that we had been wondering about. So my wife and I prepared a list of questions. Over a period of several days, my guardian angel did re-appear and answered the questions that I asked him. After each experience, I faithfully and as accurately as I possibly could typed his answers into our computer and saved them on discs.

For us, this experience has been very real. Whether this has been a series of interactive dreams, a re-occurring vision, or an actual physical appearance of a guardian angel will be left for the individual reader to decide for themselves. For the sake of the information provided, it really does not matter which method to deliver it was used what is important to remember is that angels are unable to lie and so the information given is truthful, interesting, and may help to enrich each reader's life.

PREFACE

The organization of our book is designed to tell the story of what happened to me and provide the reader with answers to a variety of questions which like us, they may have asked an angel given the opportunity to do so. The reader will also find a sampling of Bible passages that answer questions similar to those posed to my guardian angel. This procedure was used to determine whether or not my guardian angel was truly an angel giving me answers that would agree with what Holy Scriptures have to say about angels. These passages are taken from the King James version of the Holy Bible and are not meant to be all inclusive of what the Bible has to say about angels. However, enough information is provided to give someone who is not familiar with the Biblical accounts of angels to gain a good background on this subject and to provide persons who are knowledgeable about angels with an adequate review of what the Holy Scriptures say about them.

Illustrations were added to give the reader visual stimuli in the form of artists' conceptions of what angels may look like in different settings. The illustrations featuring angels are reproduced from an out-of-copyright book written in 1889 entitled: *The Beautiful Story - A Companion Book to the Holy Bible.*

The symbols of the Christian church are original drawings by Judy and Micah Smith.

The last sections of the book include a poem written by my wife during the time I was conversing with my guardian angel on a daily basis. The poem expresses her feelings of tender love toward my guardian angel and what he did for us.

She also wrote a collection of letters to the guardian angels for members of our immediate family. She basically wanted to thank each and every one of them for protecting our family members. The letters are very personal and quite moving and would serve as good examples of what you might say to your guardian angels when you want to express your gratitude for their services.

In conclusion, it is fitting to include a quote from J.W. Buel's book, *The Beautiful Story.* It reflects the purpose for the writing of *Conversations with My Guardian Angel,* and addresses this author's prayer for his fellow mankind.

"I have endeavored to so write the story that all who read it will not only gather useful lessons therefrom, but will be also stimulated to a greater interest in the Bible and a stronger love, a better faith, a more perfect obedience, and a constantly growing devotion to God, in whose service may this effort of mine lead many to enter, is the earnest prayer of the author."

DEDICATION

I am dedicating this book to my wife, Judy. She provided the motivation for me to labor with this even though our lives became extremely busy and we were not able to spend as much time interacting with each other as we normally do. She also lent her literary talents to this effort, served as proofreader, and assisted the project with her artistic talents. This is not to diminish the importance of the contributions that our son, Micah, made with his computer knowledge and skills which also made the completion of this work possible.

QUESTIONS AND ANSWERS
WITH MY
GUARDIAN ANGEL

Q. How do you know if you have a guardian angel?

A. It is very easy tell if you have a guardian angel because everyone has a guardian angel from the time that they are conceived until the time that they die.

I suppose what you really want to know is how you can reassure yourself that you really do have a guardian angel. Think back about what has happened to you in your life so far. Have you had an accident like falling down a number of steps but you did not get hurt as badly as what you could have gotten hurt. Have you been riding in a car and all of a sudden another vehicle is coming right at you but your car turns exactly the way that the other car does not turn and you avoided an accident? As a child, were you climbing into a tree when a branch broke from underneath you and as you were falling did another branch make itself available for you to grab onto. For the most part these types of happenings have good endings because a guardian angel was involved.

Q. What is God's plan for us regarding our guardian angels?

A. God's plan for you regarding your guardian angel is really quite simple. The angel is suppose to keep a steadfast watch over you and keep you as safe as possible even if you choose to do some unsafe things. Because mankind was given free wills to choose what they would be thinking and doing, angels have no control over your activities and usually do not give guidance until such time as you are in some type of danger. Guardian angels are most vigilant when you are an infant but they do continue to watch over you throughout the rest of your life.

Q. What are the duties of the guardian angels for us?

A. Their basic duty is to stay by your side for your protection. In terms of actually helping you, they must be quite creative because no two individuals are exactly alike and everyone reacts to different situations with different reactions. for instance, two fourteen year old boys may decide to go swimming in a river. As they are swimming, the current suddenly increases due to heavy rainfall upstream. The boys are both in grave danger as they become separated. For the boy who is not a strong swimmer, a log may come floating by upon which he may hang on until it reaches the bank. For the stronger swimmer, a well defined landmark may appear to which he is able to use as a guide to swim to the bank.

Q. Does everyone have a guardian angel, even people who are evil?

A. Yes, everyone has a guardian angel no matter how bad they are. God does not discriminate in providing guardian angels for any reason. He knows that even unbelievers may someday come to know Him and so they should continue to be protected.

Q. Do angels have names?

A. Each and every angel has a name. However, because there are so many billions of angels, many of the angels are named the same. God and the other angels all know each other, but sometimes you may be addressed by your name followed by the name of the person on Earth that you are serving as a guardian angel.

Q. Are females given female guardian angels and males given male guardian angels?

A. This is not so easy to answer so that you will understand it. Angels do not have a gender determination but they are given names that are generally used by males and others are given names that are frequently used by females.

There are many more male names used for angels than female names with a ratio of about two to one. For various reasons, on Earth, there tend to be more females than males, and so a female may have a guardian angel with a male or female sounding name. Males will usually have a guardian angel with a male sounding name but not always.

Q. Do angels have sexes?

A. I probably answered this already but angels are not sexed in the way humans are but we are given names that deliniate different genders.

Q. Do angels have ranks?

A. Most definitely. God's angels are very well organized not unlike the way that the ancient Romans organized their armies. There is a leader for every group of ten angels, one hundred angels, one thousand angels, ten thousand angels, one hundred thousand angels, one million angels, ten million angels, one hundred million angels, and one billion angels.

Each archangel is responsible for one billion angels and archangels are not assigned as guardian angels. If necessary, angels may be assembled in mass but they are so powerful that this is not usually done.

Q. Are angels able to communicate with each other?

A. They certainly do communicate with each other. For the most part, they discuss things within their group of ten angels. But they also talk alot with the other guardian angels in a household but they do not interfere with what those other guardian angels are doing because they are being held accountable in their own group settings by the leader of their group. Normally, angels will talk with their leader first but are allowed to speak with the leaders up the chain of command. Given the right circumstances and the importance of the particular project that they are working on an angel may communicate directly with an archangel. In my case, I am the leader of one hundred million angels and while that keeps me quite busy, it also provides me with a closer contact to the archangels. I try to do my communicating with my angel charges when the person for whom I am a guardian angel is in a safe environment.

Q. Are angels able to help each other?

A. Yes, but by and large they each stay out of each other's assignments and affairs. There is also a matter of protocal. For instance, if I know of a guardian angel who could use some assistance, I would have to contact the leaders in his chain of command and wait for them to take action or give direction. Angels usually do not ask for help but when they do, it is always provided.

Q. Do angels know the future?

A. Angels know a lot of things with their intelligence levels and memories at levels higher than humans but less than God's who is all-knowing. As much as they may want to, angels cannot tell what will happen in the future, not even one minute ahead of time.

Q. Can any human tell the future?

A. Absolutely not. They may use past factors to try to predict what may happen. Some humans are in league with devils, and the devils have convinced them that they know the future, but what they do is try to make things happen the way they said would happen.

Q. Who, then is able to tell the future?

A. Only God the Father, God the Son, and God the Holy Spirit, know exactly what is going to happen in the future.

Q. How can we better communicate with our guardian angel?

A. For the most part, try to act like an angel yourself. Do not tell lies and try to do as much good for others as you can but do not do it to puff yourself up or expect any gratitude. For thevast majority of people communication with their guardian angel is only very occasional and usually through dreams or thoughts. If your guardian angel has decided to contact you directly, it will most likely be when you are just drifting off to sleep or just beginning to awaken because this is a time when you are most likely to accept new ideas.

Q. Does it help to wear a cross, crucifix, or guardian angel pin?

A. Those are all nice pieces of jewelry and can be very attractive on you, so they may help your self-image. If you are asking does it help to wear these things in terms of protection from evil spirits, the answer is somewhat. Guardian angel pins are simply nice to wear. Devils at all levels do not like crosses or crucifixes, especially the latter.

7

Unless they are really intent on trying to do somethings, they try to avoid being around crosses and crucifixes. But, you must understand that they sometimes see these as a real challenge. For instance, one of their favorite places to tempt people is in a church that normally has a cross or crucifix. They especially delight in leading ministers away while making it look like they are doing God's work. They also really enjoy tempting the pompous Christian who thinks that he or she knows it all about religion and likes to show it off to others. Devils are well at work causing petty divisions in virtually every congregation of worshipers.

Q. When does life begin? Is abortion wrong? Why or why not?

A. Life begins at conception. Abortion is wrong because it is the murder of one of God's children. If there is a medical reason to save the life of the mother and so she could possibly have additional children, it might be considered to be all right but prayerful consideration should be given to all of the options before using abortion.

Q. If guardian angels are especially concerned with helping to protect small children, why is it that so many of them die without reaching adulthood?

A. That is a tough question but one that is asked many times. For the most part, only God knows that answer and He has not told anyone except in very special cases that archangels have brought to His attention. Sometimes it may happen so that the child does not have to suffer here on Earth. In other cases, the child is sometimes taken to his or her heavenly home because had they lived into adulthood, they would have lost faith and spent an eternity in hell. It is always difficult for the people in the child's life to accept the death but they should be reassured that there was a good reason for it even if they do not know what it was.

Q. Is homosexuality wrong? Why or why not?

For years, people have misunderstood homosexuality and they have also misinterpreted what the Holy Scriptures have to say about this through mistranslations of the original inspired Word. Homosexuality is mostly a biological condition related to the amount of hormones secreted in relationship with each of the other ones. It can also be taught in a family or social setting. Is it wrong? In my opinion, no, especially when it is caused by a hormone imbalance. Percentagewise, there are just as many if not more homosexually oriented persons entering heaven as other people. Everyone is eligible for forgiveness for everything except refusing to allow the Holy Spirit to enter their hearts. The problem here is that sexual activity outside of marriage whether it be with a person of the opposite sex, same sex, or with an animal is sinful.

Q. Wasn't Sodom and Gomorrah destroyed because the people were engaging in homosexuality?

A. Sodom and Gomorrah were destroyed because their entire populations were involved in all manner of sinfulness and no one there was a true follower of God except for Lot and his daughters.

Q. Do angels sing?

A. They most certainly do.

Q. What do they sing about and to whom?

A. Their songs are about the beauty of all created things and they are constantly giving thanks

JACOBS DREAM

to God and praising him. To be prefectly truthful, after doing this for thousands of years, it is getting difficult to

10

come up with new words and music, but we are still managing to do so. Sometimes we even borrow from the music and songs created on Earth. Some of the guardian angels have shared some of the heavenly music with the person they are serving. Most recently, this was done with Elton John.

Q. Do angels marry and have sex?

A. No, they have relationships which really cannot be described in human terms. It is a complete oneness, satisfaction, with each other and with God.

Q. Do angels sleep?

A. No, angels do not tire and there is no need for sleep.

Q. What does an angel wear?

A. That depends on what the angel is doing, but normally it is a very bright white gown. However, they wear anything that might be related to a form that they have taken for some purpose.

Q. Do angels eat?

A. No, they do not need food for nourishment.

Q. Do angels have a sense of smell?

A. Actually, they have a very acute sense of smell at a much higher level than humans.

Q. What fragrances do they like?

A. That is an interesting question because that will vary from angel to angel but for the most part angels prefer to smell things that are clean especially in a natural state. For instance, the almost nonexistant smell that could be detected from a mountain brook. Humans would think that there is no smell there.

Q. Do angels need to use money when they are on Earth?

A. Usually not, but there are some circumstances when they are in human form and need to have and use some money. For instance, if they come across a very poor family that absolutely no one else is helping, they may go to a store in human form and provide that family with life sustaining items. There is a fund of money in all of the currency forms that angels may draw from for those types of situations, but they never ever take a large sum of money to make a family rich.

Q. Do angels have to tend to personal hygiene as humans do?

A. No, they are prefectly clean at all times and sometimes this will bother some angels because they do not like to communicate with humans who are not approaching that level. For angels cleanliness is really next to Godliness.

Q. Do angels die?

A. Not in the sense that humans do. The angels have an eternal life of serving God. However, you will recall that shortly after creation, a group of angels followed Satan and rebelled and were cast out of heaven. One might consider that to be a type of death.

Q. Do all angels have wings?

A. No, this is sort of an individual taste on the part of the angels. Some prefer to have wings and others do not depending on what form they have decided to take.

Q. Do angels move about?

A. They move about a great deal and very quickly. They may be guarding their human charge, going to meet with other angels, or singing in a heavenly choir all within a few seconds.

Q. When were guardian angels and other angels created?

A. I do not know in specific years which is a measurement of time on Earth. However, the creation of angels took place before the creation of the stars, and Earth, and mankind.

Q. Do guardian angels have nationalities?

A. Now that is an interesting question. Guardian angels are assigned to different individuals with the cycle of births and deaths. An angel does not always serve someone of the same nationality but is able to take of the form of any nationality.

Q. Do I have more than one guardian angel?

A. No, everyone only has one guardian angel, but more angels can attend you if your guardian angel asks them to and they are able to leave their other duties.

Q. Do angels talk with each other?

A. Yes, I think we covered this when we talked about angels communicating with each other.

Q. Is there a Triune God?

A. Without a doubt. I know this is a concept that is virtually impossible to fully understand but it is really the case.

Q. Do angels have feelings?

A. Angels do have feelings. They feel the highest form of happiness when someone comes to accept Jesus as their personal Savior by allowing the Holy Spirit to enter into their hearts. They feel the lowest form of sorrow when a child of God loses faith and goes into the grips of the devil. They feel complete fulfilment when they are praising God.

Q. How do angels communicate with us?

A. In addition to the communicating during dreams and thoughts right before and right after sleep, angels are quite creative in how they communicate. They may cause a person to come in contact with something that they should be reading. They may guide a person's hand across a shelf of books and have the hand stop at a particular book.

GETHSEMANE.

When a book is opened or a magazine is opened, it may fall to the exact page that will help that person. Sometimes angels will appear on a television set that is already turned on and occasionally they may turn it on. Sometimes they may speak over the radio. One of my personal favorites is to turn on a light to get their attention and wonderment.

They may talk to you through a friend, relative, or spouse. In fact, their methods of communication are limitless.

Q. Do angels often appear to humans?

A. Not often, most actual appearances will come when a person has been sick for a long time and is about to die. Then his or her guardian angel may appear to them along with some other angels to give them comfort and make the transition of their soul into heaven easier. However, angels serve as God's messengers and sometimes as his administrator of judgments for individuals. In terms of frequency, this may happen three or four times during a century and the appearances may last from one day to seven days. About once every five hundred years, a visitation of major importance will take place that will last for the duration of the visited person's lifetime. Other visits and appearances of angels are very brief and usually connected with a crisis of some sort in the individual's life.

Q. When do we receive our guardian angel?

A. I think we already answered this but it is good to review it again. You receive your guardian angel at the time of conception in your mother's womb.

Q. Are our guardian angels always with us?

A. For the most part, yes, but they do leave at times to perform their heavenly duties and assist other angels or just meet with other angels. Usually, they do this at times that would be considered to be safe for the individual that they are serving.

Q. Do we have our guardian angels all of our lives?

A. Yes, all the way from conception until you take your last breath.

Q. When we die does our guardian angel help us to pass.

A. Your guardian angel is always in attendance at that time. There is nothing that the guardian angel needs to do to help you pass. On some rare occasions, a decision will have been made that it was not your time to pass, and your guardian angel will assist with directing your soul back into your body.

Q. When we die, does our guardian angel go on to a new person?

A. Yes, but it is not necessarily immediately. Sometimes there is a time span in which the guardian angel will specialize in praising God and then return to his earthly duties and become the guardian angel for a baby to be born nine months later.

Q. Are angels omnicient (all-knowing), omnipotent (all-powerful), and omnipresent (present everywhere at the same time)?

A. Angels know many things but they do not know everything. There are a good deal of things that have already happened that they were not made aware of and they certainly do not know what will happen in the future. Angels are very powerful but they do not approach the level of being all powerful. They definitely have their limitations. In terms of being everywhere, absolutely not. Angels have a well defined presence and can only be at one place at a time but they can travel very quickly. God the Father, God the Son, and God the Holy Spirit, is the only Person who is omnicient, omipotent, and omnipresent.

Q. Do humans have the ability to heal each other?

A. Only in the sense that if one human has the knowledge of how to use medicines that will cure diseases or there are certain ways to manipulate muscles, nerves, and bones that will cause a mending to take place. For instance, a dislocated shoulder can be reset and that will ultimately relieve the pain and allow for the body to heal itself. If you are talking about immediate healing from one person to another that does not place like many would have you believe. Lasting healing comes from Jesus and his healing aid may be summoned by prayer of one human for another or for one's self. Some persons are blessed with a healing warmth that will emit from their body to the body of another and it can make the other person feel better but the actual healing of the cause of the suffering must come from Jesus.

Q. Can angels heal us?

A. No, they can provide you with comfort and perhaps advise if they choose to communicate with you, but here again any real healing comes from God.

Q. Who does have the ability to heal?

A. Only God has that power and it is best to ask for the healing in Jesus' name. You must also understand that for many conditions, God created a natural healing process with blood cells to fight disease and cells that are able to be replaced.

Q. Should we pray to our guardian angel?

A. Do not even attempt to do that. It would be an insult to your guardian angel. Only direct your prayers to God the Father, God the Son, and God the Holy Spirit.

Q. Should we pray for the dead?

A. What for? The decision for salvation or no salvation has already been made for them. You should pray for the living that they may be comforted and then continue with their lives. Hopefully, they will learn from each person who has died that they need to be prepared to die at any time.

Q. Can angels communicate with animals?

A. This too is an interesting question. Angels actually can communicate with animals and animals are able to respond back in a manner that angels can understand what has been happening. The Bible gives a good example of this when Balaam's donkey was talking with an angel. If you watch your pets closely, you may notice them seemingly watching something in the air and they may be following the movements of an angel. Or they may be holding real still as if listening to something that isn't there and they might be in a period of communicating with an angel. You must understand that angels know all of the languages spoken on Earth and to understand animal talk is not that difficult once you know how.

THE ANGEL GABRIEL SPEAKING TO ZACHARIAS.

Q. Do animals have feelings?

A. Animals do have feelings but they are not as well developed as humans. They certainly feel loyalty. They have the capacity to grieve when something happens to their owner or when something happens to their own mate or another animal whom they have known. They have a feeling of being wanted. They understand love and affection. They have feelings of rejection especially if they are not cared about. They frequently have strong feelings of protection for their care provider. They also have feelings of jealousy when new animals are introduced into a home or if other animals they know are getting preferred treatment.

Q. Are there animals in heaven?

A. I really hate to be the one to tell you this because I know you are a real animal lover, but animals do not go to heaven or hell. You see they were created without souls and even with all the human traits that they sometimes take on, they cannot obtain a soul.

OH, GRAVE, WHERE IS THY VICTORY?

Q. Do angels know everything that we do?

A. Well that sort of depends on whether an angel was around when you learned about something. They must be within listening or thought receiving distance but once they learn something they do not forget it. Angels actually know much more than you do because they have been on the Earth learning more than what you have. But sometimes an angel might not know a specific thing that you know.

Q. Can angels read the thoughts of others?

A. Yes, even if the angel is not your guardian angel, the angel is able to read your thoughts when close enough to you. However, they do not have a lot of time to spend trying to listen to everyone's thoughts. They also prefer to listen to good thoughts and so they might be tuning out bad, evil, and thoughts that are in poor taste.

Q. What does an angel look like and can they change their appearances?

A. I think we discussed these questions before but I can tell you again. Angels basically can take on about any form that they want to. More often

than not, they have fair faces, flowing hair, and are attired in a bright white gowns.

Q. Can angels change form to look like a human?

A. Most definitely! This is one of their most used forms because it is less threatening to humans and if the angel must do something of a human nature then it will allow him to do that.

Q. What kind of a guardian angel is assigned to me?

A. Your guardian angel is likely to be somewhat like you but more powerful and unable to sin.

Q. How are guardian angels assigned to us?

A. God knows at the time of conception what type of person you will be, what your interests will be, and what type of an occupation you will have. The angel leaders are advised and then great care is taken to select guardian angels who will be compatable with the person whom they will be serving for a lifetime.

Q. Can angels see through walls?

A. Yes, but generally speaking, they need to be fairly close to the wall. For instance, they cannot be in New York City and see through a wall in Chicago.

Q. Can angels hear through walls?

A. Yes, but again they must be within a reasonable distance to the wall. Usually about 20 feet or so depending on the noise level in the area.

Q. Can angels go through walls?

A. Oh, that is one of their specialities. As spirits without a physical type of a body they are perfectly designed to go through walls. The problem with this is that except for their own clothing they cannot bring items with solid physical properties with them.

Q. Can we feel the presence and/or touch of an angel?

A. Many people are able to feel the presence of an angel. If you think you are one of those people, you should be feeling the presence right now because your guardian angel should be with you. However, angels have the ability to intensify their presence or lower the intensity so that at times you will be able to feel it and at other times you will not feel it. Feeling the touch of an angel is a different matter. Because they are spirits even if they would put their arm around you, you would not feel it, but of course, if the angel were appearing to you, you would see it.

Q. If my guardian angel would appear to me, could anyone else see and hear him?

A. In ninety-nine percent of the times the answer would be no. The appearance of your guardian angel is a very private matter for the angel and for you. While you might be able to see and hear the angel, no on else around you would unless the angel had some reason for allowing them to see and hear.

" For an angel went down at a certain season into the pool, and troubled the water."—JOHN v. 4.

Q. As my guardian angel, can you tell me if there is eternal life and if so, how do we receive it?

A. That is a question that you can never ask too often. There is eternal life after your death here on Earth. The problem is that eternal life exists in hell with eternal suffering as well as it exists in heaven with eternal happiness and bliss. You receive eternal life in heaven, simply by believing that Jesus Chist is your Savior and he died for you and rose again and was able to pay the penalty for all of your sins. All you have to do is make your heart and soul available for the Holy Spirit to instill this belief in you and do not reject it at any time.

Q. What about good deeds, do they get you into heaven?

A. Many people get confused about this. Good deeds proceed from people naturally after they have been saved. They are one of the immediate results

28

of accepting Christ as your Savior. To be a truly good deed, it must be performed without thought of how it could benefit you or what kind of thanks you would receive. It should also not be done to impress other people. Even all of that in place, good deeds will not in themselves get you into heaven. It cannot be stressed too much that heaven is gained by a belief and acceptance of Jesus as your Savior.

Q. Are you sure? How do we get into heaven?

A. Yes, that is right, you allow the Holy Spirit to instill the faith in you so that you accept Christ as your Savior. That's it!

Q. If there is a heaven, is there really also a hell with devils and demons?

A. By all means, hell is as real as real can be. It is not only populated by demons and devils it is ruled by Satan who was a former holy angel who rebelled and was cast out of heaven. They are very strong and do everything that they can possibly think of to acquire souls to join them. On judgment day, those souls will be reunited with their former bodies, and those people will spend their eternity in constant pain and suffering.

Q. Is there demonic possession?

A. Oh, yes, unfortunately, this is a real condition. Many people confuse this with a mental illness because it may manifest itself in such a fashion but it is quite different and very real. People who are possessed by demons should be given all the care and assistance necessary to try to rid them of these hateful creatures.

Q. What can we do to help someone who is possessed by a demon?

A. Pray constantly asking that the demon be removed. Have everyone who is of importance in that person's life join in the praying. Always ask in your prayer that Jesus Christ should remove the devil or demon. Demons do not like to be reminded of Jesus and His saving of mankind by dying on the cross. So they do not like to be in the presence of crosses and they really do not like to be in the presence of a crucifix because that is a very graphic reminder. Another physical thing that you can do is to bless some water in the name of God the Father, God the Son, and God the Holy Spirit. This simple act creates what many people call holy water. It in effect is blessed water and the devil's will recognize it as such and will try to escape from it when it is used often enough. The devils also do not like the sight of the Holy Bible especially if it is open and they know that it is being read.

Q. What can we do to avoid and protect ourselves from demons?

A. There really is not much that you can do to avoid devils and demons because there are millions of them and they are all about. They are a frequent source of temptation for just about everyone but they are especially interested in trying to beguile the believer. The best thing that you can do is to remain firm in your faith so even if you are tempted you are able to resist. It will also help to display crosses and crucifixes in your home, keep your Bibles in very visable places and read them frequently, and pray often. Regular devotions on a daily basis are an excellent idea. Also, keep your house as clean as you possibly can, angels love a clean house and devils enjoy dirt and filth.

Q. How can we protect our children from demons?

A. Be a good example for them in your faith and the exercise of your Chistian duties. Stay by your children as much as possible. Help them with their homework, tell them Bible stories, teach them to read Bible stories, play with them, eat your meals with them, pray with them, watch television with them whenever possible, and take them shopping with you. If you have to use a babysitter, make sure that the babysitter is a true believer in Christ. When they are old enough to understand, discuss demons and devils with them. Indeed, one should fear these ceatures but not be afraid to do battle with them. When they are away from home and your influence try to place them in situations that include proper supervision and if at all possible a Christian atmosphere.

Q. What does a demon look like?

A. This is a very tough question to answer because demons are able to take on many forms and they are able to change that form at will. They are very  creative in their choice of forms and may appear as angels, humans, animals, plants, and inanimate objects such as statues and automobiles. One of their very favorite things to do is to remain invisible but attempt to enter into your thought patterns especially through the form of dreams. After watching you for a while, demons are very good at understanding what a particular human likes. They look for things like whether or not the human wants a lot of money, fame, power, sexual experiences, and so forth. It is very common for a demon after determining the type of thing that a human really wants to strike up a deal for the person to obtain what he desires. This does not always involve the selling of your soul. Demons are much too clever to be that obvious. They usually start out with offers of much less consequence but ultimately the goal is to gain your soul for eternity. For instance, many crimes being committed are the result of making a deal with a demon. The demon points out all the nice things that you will be able to do with the stolen items and as his part of the deal, he guarantees that you will not get caught. This goes on from the very crude street crimes to the highly sophisticated stock fraud and computer enhanced crimes. A very frequent temptation offered is a huge sum of money to pay off gambling debts quickly. Another favorite method of appearing to people is for the demon to take on the form of another human. It is frequently as a member of the opposite sex who is very physically attractive. Still another way is to take on the appearance of a pet or possess a pet that is already owned. It can gain your trust and confidence this way and then send thought altering impulses that may make you do many things that you ordinarily would not do.

Q. Do demons visit us in the form of illnesses?

A. This is a very common form of misinformation. Diseases and illnesses have been with mankind since the fall from grace in the Garden of Eden. An illness is not a demon. But it is possible for you to become ill because of activities that you engaged in when falling under the temptational influences of a demon. Many mental illnesses mimic the symptoms of being possessed by a demon and it makes it difficult to tell the difference. The main thing to know about illnesses and demons is that when one is quite sick, it is a very vulnerable time for demons to approach you because you are physically and sometimes mentally weak at that time and perhaps more open to accepting what the demon has in mind for you.

Q. Are illnesses sent to punish us?

A. The idea that you have done soemthing terribly wrong and God has sent an illness to punish you for a particular sin or a whole life of sining is not founded on fact. Many people come to the conclusion that illness is a punishment because to them it is logical. Sometimes rather than showing care and empathy for an ill person, someone may be trying to build themselves up because what they are really thinking is,

"I am better than you are t because I am not sick." Additionally, some people actually get angry with persons who are sick because they expect them to be at their beck and call almost constantly and it cannot be done when someone is sick enough.

Q. Why are illnesses and accidents sent to us?

A. Sometimes they are sent as a test of faith or as an effort to help you to strengthen your faith. When you become quite sick or have had a serious accident it will frequently give you time to reflect on how you are living your life and you may decide to make some changes. Another explanation for why illnesses are sent does not bring pleasant thoughts to mind but it is a function of nature. Just as trees and plants are allowed to die and/or burn in forest fires to ultimately rejuvenate an area; animals and humans can reach a point at which the food supply cannot provide for them and so an illness may be sent to thin out the population to allow for stronger future generations. This is also sometimes in place at times of natural disasters such as floods, tornadoes, typhoons, hurricanes, tidal waves, and volcanic eruptions.

Q. Can guardian angels help us with our health?

A. They can be a great help in terms of providing you with additional comfort and even leading you to read various books or magazines that would be beneficial for you. If you are asking, "Are angels able to heal you?" then the answer to your question is "No!"

Q. Who can help us with our health?

A. Your bodies have been designed to heal themselves with the assistance of medicines and therapies. However, the only true healer is God Almighty, normally working through His Son Jesus Christ. Even if a Christian prays over you and a healing takes place it is not the work of the Christian but it is the work of Jesus.. I would be very suspect of a minister, faith healer, or any individual claiming to be able to heal. Even medical doctors and surgeons cannot make that claim because while they provide the vehicles of healing it is truly only God who actually heals.

Q. What is the best prayer to use?

A. Most people who are into religion and such would say that the "Lord's Prayer" is the best prayer to use in all circumstances. And that is true especially for someone who is not use to praying on a daily basis. It does have some pitfalls however. The problem is that it is used so often that many people say it without thinking about it and then it becomes a mockery rather than something that is pleasing to God. I think that the best prayer to use is the prayer of a child. When given the chance to pray on their own, the prayers of children are simple, easy to understand, and direct. In my opinion, I think God would like us to model our prayers after the prayers of children and would encourage you to make them simple and direct but most of all you must mean and believe what you are praying.

Q. Tell me, is baptism important, and if so, at what age should one be baptised?

A. Oh! Baptism is very important for a true believer. While the only criteria for obtaining salvation is a belief that Jesus has saved you, baptism is the method that God has provided to allow the Holy Spirit an opportunity to enter your willing. He uses heart which as been opened up for His acceptance this means as a reassurance that your sins have been forgiven and He will implant a faith which when nurtured and well cared for will not be shaken. Any age is the correct age to be baptised but it is very important to do it as soon after birth as you can to start an infant on his or her way to salvation. There is absolutely nothing wrong with being baptised over and over again throughtout your life. You can only benefit from continued visits from the Holy Spirit.

Q. Is the Lord's Supper or Holy Communion important and why?

A. This practice was created or instituted by Jesus himself. He did this so that believers would have a physical rememberance of what He did for them with his suffering and death. By drinking His blood and eating his body, believers are reminded in a dramatic fashion how Christ gave them the ultimate gift of salvation and it also provides them with another means of obtaining forgiveness of their sins. Sometimes Christians view the taking of Holy Communion as a renewal of their baptisimal vows and that is a God pleasing viewpoint. How often should you take Holy Communion is an individual matter and it does not make a lot of sense to stipulate a certain number of times as some organized churches have done. I realize that some religious leaders even with the stature of Martin Luther were prone to set a minimum number of times that one should commune, but those thoughts were not given by divine inspiration.

Q. Is there reincarnation?

A. This is a very interesting idea but if you think about this in logical terms you will see that it is almost impossible. When a person dies, his body remains here on Earth and his soul goes to heaven to wait until Judgment Day arrives. Let us say tht reincarntion takes place and the soul leaves heaven and takes up residence in another human body. Given an average lifespan of 70 years, this type of a transfer could happen ten to fifteen times during a century. Even by conservative estimates the Earth has been in existence for at least 60 centuries which means that one soul could have inhabited 600 to 900 bodies during that time. On Judgment Day, which body would be reunited with the soul for eternity? The answer to the question appears to be no.

Q. Is there really a heaven?

A. There is most certainly a heaven but you must accept that concept on faith.

Q. Where is it?

A. In the universe, but just outside of man's view even with the most powerful telescopes and rocket probes. However, it is a very short distance in terms of time that it takes to transport souls and angels.

Q. Are we truly forgiven for our sins?

A. You may rest peacefully every night knowing that your sins have been completely forgiven. Even though you may feel that you are not worthy of such treatment your sins have been completely atoned for you.

Q. How do we receive forgiveness for our sins?

A. This is so easy that many people fail to grasp it. You accept Jesus Christ as your Savior and your sins will be forgiven for you. That's it.

Q. Is one religion favored over another in God's eyes?

A. In my opinion, no, He seems to dislike them all. Even the ones that profess to be founded on the blood of Jesus Christ and whose followers are called Christians are no longer doing God's bidding. They are not so concerned about saving souls as they are about their real estate holdings, whether or not their hospitals are turning good profits, or their schools have good athletic teams. Putting it in human terms, God is extremely disappointed that the various denominations are bogged down with their own sense of importance and bickering about inspiration of Scripture, when one should baptise, when confirmation should be provided, what criteria is needed for membership in a church, and should one be married or buried from a church of which he or she was not a member. As the list goes on and on, and this is so ridiculous that it puts all of them out of God's favor.

Q. What do you think concerning the "theory of evolution?"

A. If you define evolution as change occurring over a period of time within a race or nationality of persons, or within a species of animals or plants, then I would say that evolution does indeed take place to a degree. Just as example, look what a change in dietary habits can do for new generations who started in underdeveloped countries. They will generally gain in height, weight, and intelligence among other things. If by evolution, you are talking about the beginning of life and the transformation that may have taken place in which man did not exist but came from an animal background, then the theory is not correct. All creatures and plants were created by God at the beginning of time. Yes, by selective breeding and experimentation variations of plants and animals that did not exist previously now inhabit the Earth, but these are virtually minor changes rather than an evolutionary process.

Q. What do you know about so called faith healers such as Benny Hinn?

A. Jesus, the Son of God, is the ONLY Person who can perform miracles and actually heal someone. If a true believer prays and calls upon Jesus to perform a healing and the individual to be healed also has true faith, one might say that a faith healing takes place. However, the person doing the praying can never take credit for the healing of any kind.

There are three levels of faith healers. The first level is a true believer who attributes the healings to Christ. The second level which includes many of the persons claiming to be faith healers are nothing but con-artists who want to be well paid through contributions preferably in cash. They go to great lengths to put on elaborate religious shows in person and on television but their healings are generally staged in some fashion. They may have persons planted in the audience who pretend to be sick or injured and then are immediately cured on cue. They may use a system of false testimonials that are read over the air to make you believe that you could be healed by listening and/or touching your television set. One of the very successful cons involved here are people who think they are sick and then believe that this procedure heals them and they are so thankful that they send in lots of money.

Still another method is to receive letters from people indicating their particular illness and then responding to them with form letters saying that prayers have been offered for them and a healing is taking place. The third type of faith healing originates from Satan. He works through mediums such as fortune tellers, psychics, and witches. A promise of health and cures for certain illnesses may be given in exchange for ones soul. Money may also be extracted for these services but of course, the greatest price is the payment of ones soul resulting in eternal damnation in exchange for short-lived comfort here on Earth.

Q. Do near death experiences exist and what do you think about them?

A. Yes, they do exist. They are most likely to occur after a serious accident which is life threatening. Unfortunately, there are not as many as what you might think because people sort of get caught up into this and report having a near death experience even when they have not had one. They may have had a dream that resembles a near death experience and they are not able to separate the two. On the other hand, they may be searching for attention and they know that if they make up a story involving a near death experience others will probably listen and have sympathy for them. Some people do it for money because if it is believable enough they may be able to sell their story.

Q. What do we feel when we die?

A. I really do not know the answer to that but I can give you my opinion. Depending on the type of death you could feel all sorts of emotions right before it happens. Those feelings would vary from extreme fear to great happiness depending upon how you view the after life and whether or not you are prepared. I would think that the absolute best type of death would be when one dies in their sleep because there would be no apprehension one way or the other. If you are asking, what do you feel at the exact moment of death, I would think that you do not feel anything at all because your mind stops working. Your soul leaving your body is probably not felt by your body because it occurs at that moment of death.

Q. Do we see departed loved ones when we are d
we die?

A. There are many reports of people seeing departed loveu ᵕ
shortly before they die themselves. To actually see a
departed loved one, I do not think is possible. However, it is
very likely that an image of a loved one is seen that is
projected in your mind briefly before you die. You must
understand that the physical body of your loved one is
resting somewhere on or in the earth. His or her soul is in
storage in heaven or hell and will not be reunited until the
last day. But it is possible for your mind to allow you to
picture what you think your loved one now looks like.

Q. Do we see God?

A. No, no man sees God as He is. He would have to change
into a form that you could stand to view. While anything is
possible with God, He normally communicates with
individuals through their guardian angels.

Q. Do we see bright lights and a tunnel when we die?

A. There certainly are enough reports from individuals who
have experienced a near death happening that bright lights

and a tunnel are seen. Personally, I have not seen it but it would make sense that a type of pathway or conduit for souls to travel to their temporary resting places does exist and in all likelihood it is well lighted if that resting place is in heaven.

Q. Do departed loved ones help us in the process of dying?

A. No, they are not aware of what is happening to you while you have been left behind on Earth. Even though some people may dream or think that departed loved ones have come back in spirit to help them that is only the imagination portion of the individual who is getting ready to die.

Q. Who does help us in the process of dying?

A. You basically help yourself to get ready but the Holy Spirit is also making final attempts to make sure that you really and truly have faith and have accepted Jesus Christ as your Saviour and that you are not just saying that. Your guardian angel may also be assisting you to prepare your for death. Your angel may even appear to your shortly before your death occurs, and if you find this happening, you should be leaving your heart wide open to receive the Holy Spirit for the final time.

Q. Does our life pass before us as we are dying?

A. It depends on the circumstances. If you die in your sleep, I would say no. If you are in a situation in which you know that you will be dying shortly, then yes. For instance, if you are in a car that was driven into a deep river and it is filling with water you would have time for a replay of your life, or if you were in an airplane and it was falling from the sky for several minutes you would also have time. You do not have to be dying to have your life reviewed in your mind. This actually takes place frequently but in brief segments whenever you are experiencing a memory.

Q. Is each person's death an individual experience or does everyone have the same experience?

A. Again, this is my opinion, but it seems that the actual moment of death for everyone is the same. When the soul departs is a different experience for persons because the soul is leaving for heaven or for hell. The types of feelings and things that one would go through as they are approaching death must be on an individualized basis depending on how the death is occurring and the mental preparations that a person has made in advance.

Q. Could you tell us anything else about the process of dying?

A. Of all the things feared by man death is the most prevalent and greatest fear.   Even when completely prepared and confident that one will be saved there is still an element of anxiety and fear that will not go away until the death occurs. If you want to think about death from a psychological point of view, it would be the strongest of all phobias. The fear in a person especially one who is not saved can be so great that it actually can bring on a tightness that will hasten death.

Q. What is a soul?

A. Humans have a very difficult time understanding the concept of a soul. Attempts have been made to see it, hear it, and weigh it. A soul is an entity that has to be accepted with faith that it exists. It is the embodiment of ones self which means that it is the life force that keeps a being living.

Q. Where does your soul go when you die?

A. Ultimately it goes to rest until Judgment Day comes, within a place set aside for souls in heaven or in hell. However, in many cases the movement of the soul to these temporary resting places may take days or months but it could also be immediate. It is not uncommon for a soul to drift on Earth visiting places where a departed one has lived or spent time before it makes that final transition.

Q. Are marriages made in heaven?

A. For the most part the answer would be no. Humans are permitted to exercise their free wills and this extends to choosing their own mates. If you are asking does God know who you are going to marry then the answer is yes because He knows everything even though everything does not please Him. However on very rare occasions, God uses his angels to influence their human charges to behave in such a fashion that their paths will cross the path of their intended mate. While the humans involved are still exercising their free wills, the conditions in which they find themselves are such that it would be difficult for them not to join with each other in marriage. The reason that this is done is that one or both of the marriage partners is to do something substancial with their lives and he or she will require the strong support and assistance from this particular mate. There are some prime examples of this happening during Biblical times such as Abraham and Sarah, Mary and Joseph, and Elizabeth and Zechariah. Other persons in this category would include

Martin Luther and his wife Katherine, and Harry Truman and his wife Bess.

Q. Does the Lord have a plan for our lives?

A. He certainly does have a plan for each human and that is for each person to believe on the Lord Jesus Christ and be saved.   Unfortunately, with the free will of mankind, combined with the work of Satan and his legions of devils, that plan is not carried out frequently enough. If you are asking what occupation a person will be going into, how big his family will be and things like that the answer is God has known everything since the beginning of time.   However, again, man has his own free will and he chooses.

Q. Is there such a thing as destiny?

A. Many people think that you are predestined to do something and so they assume an attitude of whatever is going to happen will happen and I cannot do anything about it. That really is not the case, every man and woman has control over their own lives with the restraints of their family, living conditions, and particular government among other factors. Here again, God does know what is going to happen but He only rarely will have an angel involved in seeing to it that things take place properly.

Q. What do you think is the most important lesson that mankind has to learn?

A. Each individual man and woman must learn not to rely on themselves for salvation. All the success possible in life in terms of fame and fortune will not achieve the ultimate goal of eternal life for you. In very practical terms, the most important thing that mankind should learn is to be a believer and live in the world but not be of the world. This is extremely difficult but very necessary.

Q. Should information about our lives be sought through psychics, mediums, fortune tellers, or clarvoiants?

A. If you are at a party or just at home and playing a game based on this format, it might be all right for its entertainment value. However, if you are doing this for real, it is very dangerous because even if these people are only fraudulant and trying to get your money and or property it can cause you a lot of grief. Even worse is when they are in league with Satan and his forces and then become a method for him to get a foothold in your life. While men and women sin frequently, they should not be doing it on purpose. The problem here is that many psychics, witches, mediums, fortune tellers, and clarvoiants use the name of God in their practices and this is taking the name of God in vain which is a well defined sin that can be easily avoided.

Q. How do I go about finding a real Christian church to attend?

A. Most people would say visit a church during services on several occasions and see if God's Word is being taught in it's truth and purity. What you really would have to do is visit with some of the members when they are at home and at work. Listen carefully to what they say especially about each other and the leaders of their church, you will soon discover how Christian it really is. Visit with the pastor of the church in several settings including church meetings and social affairs in addition to talking with him or her privately. Try to ascertain whether or not his main focus is caring for his flock and seeking out the sheep who are lost or are his primary concerns centered about how much money he can raise, how he knows almost everything, how he treats persons who seek his aid and may or may not be members who contribute to his church, and how he lives his own life when he thinks no one else can see him. I can tell you that I have been in many congregations and they have been of various denominations, and I have not found a single one in which power struggles have not been going on and plans are being made with results to glorify the men and women making the arrangements rather than to the praise and honor of God. Much lip service is given to the preaching and teaching of the Word of God, but genuine sincerity is lacking. You should attend church and honor the Sabbath Day and this will give you an opportunity to praise God on your own but finding a true Christian church to attend will be next to impossible.

Q. Do you feel that there soon will be cures for some of the serious diseases?

A. Mankind has been blessed with a rather high level of intelligence and the capacity to do good. Current research and the development of effective procedures to treat diseases is at its highest level ever. So, yes, cures for some of the serious diseases will be found. The sad part of this is that when cures are found greed enters into the minds of the persons and companies able to provide those cures and many of the people who so desperately need the cure are left out because they cannot afford it. Ideally, medical care should be free to everyone in the world but that is not likely to come to pass. It is more likely that new diseases will appear and old one may resurface.

Q. When we die is there the possibility of us becoming an angel?

A. No, angels were created at the beginning of time and the number is constant. No matter how good they are on Earth, humans do not become angels.

Q. Do you feel there will be world peace?

A. In my opinion, there will never be total peace throughout the world. I base my opinion on past history and there has never been a time of total peace. The prophecies that you find in the Holy Scriptures also indicate that there will always be wars and rumors of war and it is a sign of the final coming when God will come back to the Earth and take His faithful with him to their heavenly homes.

Q. Why are the Ten Commandments so important for us?

A. The Ten Commandments are basically God's gift to mankind in the form of the best way that they could live their lives. Within the Ten Commandments you will find everything necessary for treating yourself and your neighbor well as well as establishing your proper relationship with God. Man has made this so complicated. The millions upon millions of pages of laws that man has instituted are all unnecessary if everyone would simply obey the Ten Commandments in spirit and letter. They are extremely important for you. If you try your very best to keep them, you will gain the respect of yourself and the other humans with whom you come into contact. You will also please God with your attempts to obey and He understands that you cannot keep them perfectly and that is why He has arranged for your continuous forgiveness.

Q. Are there just a certain number of souls?

A. Yes, there is one soul for every person who has ever been conceived or ever will be conceived between the time that man was created until the time that Judgment Day arrives. That number reaches into the trillions upon trillions and while it is an exact number I cannot tell you what it is because I do not know how many babies will have been conceived by the end of time.

Q. How best can we teach our children so that they will know salvation?

A. The key word in your question is "teach." You must understand that salvation for your children is a private matter between them and the Holy Spirit. However, it is your duty as parents to provide every opportunity possible for them to accept Jesus as their Savior. The best possible way for you to teach children to be open for salvation is to set a good example yourself. Do not hide your faith under a basket, but let it shine to them on a daily basis, twenty-four hours a day, seven days a week, for the entire time that your children, grandchildren, and great-grandchildren are with you. The first thing that you should do in a physical sense is to have them baptised as soon as possible.

This should be followed by reading to them everyday for years about things that happened as they are recorded in the Bible. The stories that you read to them or tell them should be at a level that they will understand. When they get old enough to read on their own they should be encouraged to study these lessons by themselves. But you should also continue to read and talk to them. When their understanding matures, you should take much time to have discussions about what they and you are learning. You should view teaching your children about God's plan for salvation as the primary goal for your life. In these times, there really is no excuse for not instructing your children because materials are so available from your bank of knowledge, in books, on tape, on compact discs, and in video formats.

Q. Are people born with certain talents? If so, how can we find out what talents these are and how can we best use them?

A. Yes, people are born with certain talents and also tendencies to acquire particular skills easier than others. Your modern day psychologists refer to this as having multiple intelligences. Every person has a different combination of talent and potential development for such things as music, art, reading, math, logical thinking, ability to sequence, organizational skills, people relating skills, and so forth, the list is almost endless. You find out what talents that you have by being willing to try different things and you will learn what you are good at and then you can develop refined skills in those areas. You should place yourself and your children in as many, hopefully safe, settings as you can so that you are able to find your talents. The best use of your talents is to use them to do God pleasing things. This does not mean that you have to be directly involved in the spreading of the Gospel; etc. What it does mean is that you must use your talents to the fullest of their potential to the service of others, your family members, and yourself. Keep in mind that this is a lifelong search to find your talents and make use of them.

Q. How long has the Earth been in existence?

A. Not as long as what many people think. Time does not mean much to me, but in human terms of calculating years, the Earth has been in existence for less than ten thousand years.

Q. Do humans have auras? If so, what does this mean?

A. Humans in amongst themselves do not have auras that surround them. But auras do exist. Auras are inner feelings that appear to be caused by airborn conditions. For instance, you can walk into a room of strangers and feel a sense of tension, happiness, friendliness, anxieity, etc. Sometimes auras are sent to warn of impending dangers and it is wise to pay attention to them because you may be able to take action in time that will avoid the danger. If you would like to experience an aura without being in danger, you might try going to a cemetery late at night all by yourself and stand for a few moments at the center point of the cemetery. The feeling that you get, if not a true aura would closely duplicate one.

Q. Are some people clairvoyant or have e.s.p.?

A. Some people do have a natural intuition about other people and things. Some experiments have been conducted and over a period of many trials, some people have been able to choose thoughts and so forth at a rate greater than the laws of chance would have predicted. However, this is restricted to what is going on in the present and not the future. No one knows what is in the future except for God. That means no men, no women, no angels, no devils know what the future will bring. However, it is a favorite trick that devils play convincing someone that they will be able to have super powers and predict the future. On the other hand, some people appear to be blessed with the ability to know what has happened in the past even without being there. Because angels and devils both have good memories and have been here since creation it is possible for them to convey information to certain persons. Because angels and devils cannot be present everywhere they sometimes have to seek out some of their counterparts and get the information from them.

Q. Do angels have telekinetic powers?

A. Yes, and they make use of them. They have been known to use their thought processes to loosen chains that are binding prisoners unjustly restrained or being persecuted for their beliefs. They have also been known to push a foot off of an accelerator at an appropriate time to prevent an accident. They have been known to move rocks and prevent someone from falling over a cliff. They have been known to fell a tree so that it falls into the rushing water of a flood swollen stream and provide a person trapped in the swirling water with something to hang onto.

Q. Do some people have telekinetic powers?

A. Not really, human brains are not that highly developed even at the super genius level. What actually is taking place is that someone may be in touch with their guardian angel or they may be in touch with a devil and it will appear that the human is making something move but in fact it is a spirit acting from another dimension.

Q. What is heaven like?

A. It is so beautiful that it cannot be explained in words used by humans. An adjective simply does not exist that can adequately describe heaven. Everyone has a different idea of what a beautiful scene heaven is but if you would take your favorite scene in nature and make it one hundred times as beautiful as it is, then it might be one tenth as beautiful as heaven.

Q. What do you know of hell?

A. I have never been there, and I will never go there so I do not know exactly what it is like. I have heard that it is so hot that a person will feel that he or she is being burned constantly without any form of relief, not even a single drop of water.

Q. Do ghosts exist?

A. Not really, what are commonly thought of as ghosts are actually some devils playing some tricks to disguise themselves.

Q. Are there spirits that walk the earth not being able to go to their eternal rest?

A. This again is a cruel trick. Some devils take on the forms and characteristics of recently or not so recently humans who have died and then they decide to "haunt" a particular building or locale.

Q. Why is it that some of the departed do not depart immediately but remain on earth for a period of time?

A. I think you are asking why a soul may not go immediately to heaven to rest until Judgment Day. Sometimes an individual especially a parent has such a great love for their children that they have a difficult time leaving and so they stay around for a while but ultimately make the journey. This is also known to happen between husbands and wives who have a great love for each other. Other examples are close friends who sometimes will do this.

Q. How many souls are there?

A. I already answered this.

Q. What is an approximate number of people who will actually be going to heaven?

A. This is rather sad, but at the current rate, it would appear that by the end of time the number will be less than one million. Through the ages, billions of persons have professed to be true believers but they have let other things get in their way especially the love of money and material items and they will not be making it for an eternally joyful life in heaven.

BIBLICAL PROOFS FOR ANGELS
AND THEIR ACTIVITIES

I am by nature a "Doubting Thomas." Basically, I question all information that I read, hear, or observe. This type of an attitude is actually quite useful in my chosen profession of being an educational psychologist and consultant as the major aspect of my work involves the analyzing of data, drawing conclusions, and then providing others with advice. I was able to readily accept having a dream about my guardian angel; however, when he appeared to me and was willing to answer questions and engage in conversations over an extended period of time, I had to question what was taking place. I have been a student of the Holy Bible since the age of six and certainly was acquainted with the concept of angels, but I had never envisioned such a close and personal genuine experience, I sought the advice of our local pastor and a professor of religion at a nearby university who is a recognized authority on angels and demons. After hearing the details of my experiences with a spiritual being, the pastor and professor gave me similar advice. They said that I needed to compare what my angel told me to what is recorded in Holy Scriptures and if no disagreement could be found, I could be certain that I had been visited by my guardian angel.

I prepared another list of questions that could be used to make a comparison to what my guardian angel had said and then looked for the anwers in the Holy Scriptures. Here are the questions and the Biblical responses that I found.

When were angels created?

Praise ye the Lord. Praise ye the Lord from the heavens: Praise Him in the heights. Praise ye Him, all his angels: Praise ye Him, all his hosts. Praise ye Him, sun and moon; praise Him all ye stars of light. Praise Him, ye heavens of heavens, and ye waters that be above the heavens. Let them praise the name of the Lord; for He commanded, and they were created. Psalm 148: 1-5.

For by Him were all things created, that are in heaven, and that are in earth, visible and invisible, whether they be thrones, or dominions, or principalities, or powers: all things were created by Him, and for Him. Colossians 1: 16.

In the beginning God created the heaven and the earth. Genesis 1: 1.

For in six days the Lord made heaven and earth, the sea, and all that in them is, and rested the seventh day: wherefore the Lord blessed the sabbath day, and hallowed it. Exodus 20: 11.

How many angels are there?

And he said, The Lord came from Sinai, and rose up from Seir unto them; he shined forth from Mount Paran, and he came with ten thousands of saints (holy angels); from his right hand went a firery law for them. Deuteronomy 33: 02.

A fiery stream issued and came forth from before him; thousand thousands ministered unto him, and ten thousand times ten thousand stood before him: the judgment was set, and the books were opened. Daniel 7: 10.

But ye are come unto mount Sion, and unto the city of the living God, the heavenly Jerusalem, and to an innumerable company of angels, Hebrews 12: 22.

Do angels appear resembling men?

And there came two angels to Sodom at even; and Lot sat in the gate of Sodom; and Lot seing them rose up to meet them; and he bowed himself with his face toward the ground; and he said, Behold now, my lords, turn in, I pray you, into your servant's house, and tarry all night, and wash your feet, and ye shall rise up early, and go on your ways. And they said, Nay; but we will abide in the street all night. And he pressed upon them greatly; and they turned in unto him, and entered into his house; and he made them a feast, and did bake unleavened bread, and they did eat. Genesis 19: 1-3.

And the men said unto Lot, Hast thou here any besides? Son-in-law, and thy sons, and thy daughters, and whatsoever thou hast in the city, bring them out of this place. ... And when the morning arose, then the angels hastened Lot, saying, Arise, take thy wife, and thy two daughters, which are here; lest thou be consumed in the iniquity of the city. Genesis 19: 12 & 15.

Do angels appear in dreams?

And Jacob went out from Beersheba, and went toward Haran. And he lighted upon a certain place, and tarried there all night, because the sun was set; and he took of the stones of that place, and put them for his pillows, and lay down in that place to sleep. And he dreamed, and behold a ladder set up on earth, and the top of it reached to heaven: and behold the angels of God ascending and descending on it. And, behold, the Lord stood above it, and said, I am the Lord God of Abraham thy father, and the God of Isaac: the land whereon thou liest, to thee will I give it, and to thy seed. Genesis 28: 11-13.

Do angels have emotions?

When the morning stars sang together, and all the sons of God (heavenly beings) shouted for joy? Job 38: 7.

Either what woman having ten pieces of silver, if she lose one piece, doth not light a candle, and sweep the house, and seek diligently till she find it? And when she hath found it, she calleth her friends and her neighbors together, saying, Rejoice with me; for I have found the piece which I had lost. Likewise, I say unto you, there is joy in the presence of the angels of God over one sinner that repenteth. Luke 15: 8-10.

Then the angel of the Lord answered and said, O Lord of hosts, how long wilt thou not have mercy on Jerusalem and on the cities of Judah, against which thou has had indignation these threescore and ten years? And the Lord answered the angel that talked with me with good words and comfortable words. Zechariah 1: 12-13.

Do angels worship God?

In the year that king Uzziah died I saw also the Lord sitting upon a throne, high and lifted up, and his train filled the temple. Above it stood the seraphims; each one had six wings, with twain he covered his face, and with twain he covered his feet, and with twain he did fly. And one cried unto another, and said, Holy, holy, holy, is the Lord of hosts; the whole earth is full of his glory. And the posts of the door moved at the voice of him that cried, and the house was filled with smoke. Then said I, Woe is me! For I am undone; because I am a man of unclean lips, and I dwell in the midst of a people of unclean lips; for mine eyes have seen the King, the Lord of hosts. Then flew one of the seraphims unto me, having a live coal in his hand, which he had taken with the tongs from off the altar: And he laid it upon my mouth, and said, Lo, this hath touched thy lips; and thy sin purged. Also I heard the voice of the Lord saying, Whom shall I send, and who will go for us? Then said I, Here am I, send me.

Isaiah 6: 1-8.

Do angels forewarn and instruct humans?

And being warned of God in a dream that they should not return to Herod, they departed into their own country another way. And when they were departed, behold, the angel of the Lord appeareth to Joseph in a dream, saying, Arise, and take the young child and his mother, and flee into Egypt, and be thou there until I bring thee word: for Herod will seek the young child to destroy him. Matthew 2: 12-13.

But when Herod was dead, behold, an angel of the Lord appeareth in a dream to Joseph in Egypt, Saying, Arise, and take the young child and his mother, and go into the land of Israel: for they are dead which sought the young child's life. And he arose, and took the young child and his mother, and came into the land of Israel. Matthew 2: 19-21.

Do angels execute God's judgments upon people?

The Son of man shall send forth his angels, and they shall gather out of his kingdom all things that offend, and them which do iniquity; And shall cast them into a furnace of fire; there shall be wailing and gnashing of teeth. Matthew 13: 41-42.

So shall it be at the end of the world; the angels shall come forth, and sever the wicked from among the just, And shall cast them into the furnace of fire: there shall be wailing and gnashing of teeth. Matthew 13: 49-50.

Did angels minister to Jesus when He was on the Earth?

Then the devil taketh him (Jesus) up into the holy city, and setteth him on a pinnacle of the temple. And saith unto him, if thou be the Son of God, cast thyself down: for it is written: "He shall give his angels charge concerning thee and in their hands they shall bear thee up, lest at any time thou dash thy foot against a stone." Jesus said unto him, "It is written again, Thou shalt not tempt the Lord thy God. Again, the devil taketh him up into an exceeding high mountain, and sheweth him all the kingdoms of the world, and the glory of them; And saith unto him, All these things will I give thee, if thou wilt fall down and worship me. Then saith Jesus unto him, "Get thee hence, Satan: for it is written, Thou shalt worship the Lord thy God, and him only shalt thou serve." Then the devil leaveth him, and behold, angels came and ministered unto him. Matthew 4: 5-11.

And he came out, and went, as he was wont, to the Mount of Olives; and his disciples also followed him. And when he was at the place, he said unto them, "Pray that ye enter not into temptation." And he was withdrawn from them about a stone's cast, and kneeled down, and prayed. Saying, "Father, if thou be willing, remove the cup from me; nevertheless, not my will, but thine be done." And there appeared an angel unto him from heaven, strengthening him. And being in an agony he prayed more earnestly: and his sweat was as it were great drops of blood falling down to the ground. Luke 22: 39-44.

Do angels tell us about future events?

For there stood by me this night the angel of God, whose I am, and whom I serve, Saying, Fear not, Paul; thou must be brought before Caesar: and, lo, God hath given thee all them that sail with thee. Wherefore, sirs, be of good cheer; for I believe God, that it shall be even as it was told me. Howbeit we must be cast upon a certain island. Acts 27: 23-26.

Do we have guardian angels?

For he shall give his angels charge over thee, to keep thee in all thy ways. Psalms 91: 11.

Take heed that ye despise not one of these little ones; for I say unto you, That in heaven their angels do always behold the face of my Father which is in heaven. For the Son of man is come to save that which was lost. Matthew 18: 10-11.

Do angels assist people with physical help?

Then said Daniel unto the king, O king, live for ever. My God hath sent his angel, and hath shut the lions' mouths that they have not hurt me forasmuch as before him innocency was found in me; and also in thee, O king, have I done no hurt. Daniel 6: 21-22.

Therefore sent he thither horses, and chariots, and a great host: and they came by night, and compassed the city about. And when he servant of the man of God was risen early, and gone forth, behold, an host compassed the city both with horses and chariots. And his servant said unto him, Alas, my master, how shall we do? And he answered, Fear not, for they that be with us are more than they that be with them. And Elisha prayed, and said, Lord, I pray thee, open his eyes, that he may see. And the Lord opened the eyes of the young man; and he saw; and behold, the mountain was full of horses and chariots of fire round about Elisha. II Kings 6: 14-17.

And when Herod would have brought him forth, the same night Peter was sleeping between two soldiers, bound with two chains: and the keepers before the door kept the prison. And, behold, the angel of the Lord came upon him, and a light shined in the prison; and he smote Peter on the side, and raised him up, saying, Arise up quickly. And his chains fell off from his hands. And the angel said unto him, Gird thyself, and bind on thy sandals. And so he did. And he saith unto him, Cast thy garment about thee, and follow me. And he went out, and followed him; and wist not that it was true which was done by the angel; but thought he saw a vision. When they were past the first and second ward, they came unto the iron gate that leadeth unto the city; which opened to them of its own accord: and they went out, and passed on through one street; and forthwith the angel departed from him. And when Peter was come to himself, he said, Now I know of a surety, that the Lord hath sent his angel, and hath delivered me out of the hand of Herod, and from all the expectation of the people of the Jews. Acts 12: 6-11.

Do angels have intelligence?

To fetch about this form of speech hath thy servant, Joab, done this thing; and my lord is wise, according to the wisdom of an angel of God, to know all things that are in the earth. II Samuel 14: 20.

Do angels have limits to their knowledge and intelligence?

"Verily I say unto you, This genertion shall not pass, till all these things be fulfilled. Heaven and earth shall pass away, but my words shall not pass away. But of that day and hour knoweth no man, no, not the angels of heaven, but my Father only. Matthew 24: 34-36.

Should we pray to or worship angels?

And I John saw these things, and heard them. And when I had heard and seen, I fell down to worship before the feet of the angel which shewed me these things. Then saith he unto me, See thou do it not: for I am thy fellow-servant, and of thy brethren the prophets, and of them which keep the sayings of this book: worship God. Revelation 22: 8-9.

Do angels minister to people?

But to which of the angels said he at any time, Sit on my right hand, until I make thine enemies thy footstool? Are they not all ministering spirits, sent forth to minister for them who shall be heirs of salvation? Hebrews 1: 13-14.

Are angels strong and powerful?

And it came to pass that night, that the angel of the Lord went out, and smote in the camp of the Assyrians an hundred fourscore and five thousand: and when they arose early in the morning, behold, they were all dead corpses. II Kings 19: 35.

Do demons (devils) sometimes present themselves as angels?

Beloved, believe not every spirit, but try the spirits whether they are of God: because many false prophets are gone out into the world. Hereby know ye the Spirit of God: Every spirit that confesseth that Jesus Christ is come in the flesh is of God: And every spirit that confesseth not that Jesus Christ is come in the flesh is not of God: and this is that spirit of antichrist, whereof ye have heard that it should come; and even now already is it in the world. Ye are of God, little children, and have overcome them: because greater is he that is in you, than he that is in the world.

They are of the world: therefore speak they of the world, and the world hearth them. We are of God: he that knoweth God heareth us; he that is not of God heareth not us. Hereby know we the spirit of truth, and the spirit of error. I John 4: 1-6.

Do angels assist us in death?

And it came to pass, that the beggar died, and was carried by the angels into Abraham's bosom: the rich man also died, and was buried; Luke 16: 22.

Do angels assist men and women of God in their efforts to spread the good news of the gospel?

Then the high priest rose up, and all they that were with him, (which is the sect of the Sadducees), and were filled with indignation, And laid their hands on the apostles, and put them in the common prison. But the angel of the Lord by night opened the prison doors, and brought them forth, and said, Go, stand and speak in the temple to the people all the words of this life. And when they heard that, they entered into the temple early in the morning, and taught. Acts 5: 17-21.

ARTHUR'S ANGEL

BY

JUDY SMITH

Angel dear, sent from heaven up above,
Here to love
and guide me
With all your perfect love

Dressed in gown of shining white
With features fair
and flowing hair,
You guard me with delight.

God in His wisdom sent to everyone
An angel, full of love,
To guard and guide us
To our heavenly home above.

Thank you, Lord, for your love
And your tender care
And thank you, Lord, for my angel
So beautiful and fair.

JUDY'S LETTERS TO OUR

FAMILY GUARDIAN ANGELS

To my dear angel Jonquil,

From the moment when my life began, the dear Lord gave me you, Jonquil, to be my guardian angel. You have been with me now for over 50 years. As a baby and young child you were my watchful babysitter. You saw me through all my school years and walked along side me on my way to school. For many years, when my mom was so seriously ill you helped me get through that difficult time in my life. When I met the love of my life, Arthur, and married him, you shared my happiness.

When I was pregnant with my first child, Shawn, you saw me through his difficult delivery to a joyous birth. As a young wife and mother, you helped me with many difficulties and trials. My joys and happiness were also yours.

You saw my marriage constantly strengthen, grow and deepen in love. You've seen me in bad times and good.

The blessing of my second child, Micah, surely made you as happy as it made me.

As illnesses were present in my life, so were you to protect me from them, and to see me through them.

I hope that through the years you have been proud of me. I've always tried to do my best.

Words of thank you seem to be so inadequate to say how much you mean to me and how much I love you for all that you've done for me.

I must thank my dear Lord Jesus, for loving me so very much as to give me a guardian angel like you. He is and has been so wonderful, glorious and merciful to me. Thank you, God, with all of my heart. And thank you, Jonquil, for being such a special guardian angel, and for being such an important part of my life.

Your loving charge,
Judy

Dear Angel David,

You are the guardian angel of our first grandson, Devin Michael. He was born February 16, 1991. Please keep this wonderful boy in your tender care, always guiding him toward eternal life in heaven with his loving Father.

Thank you, dear David, for Devin's care.

Devin's loving grandmother,
Judy

Dear Angel Ariel,

Our granddaughter, Autum Rhea is your charge. She was born September 17, 1992. A fair-haired little beauty. She is in need of all of your love and guidance. Lead her to her final distination in heaven with her Lord, Jesus Christ.

Thank you, Ariel, for your tender care of Autum.

Autum's loving grandmother,
Judy

Dear Angel Jonathan,

Seth Gabriel, our youngest grandson, enjoys your loving guardianship. He was born September 2, 1994. Always protect this dear little one, keeping him in your loving watch at all times. Lead him with your guiding hand to life eternal with the Lord.

Thank you, Jonathan, for your special care of Seth.

Seth's loving grandmother,
Judy

Dear Angel John,

My first child, Shawn Michael, is your loving charge. I can't express the excitement and anticipation I felt at the birth of my first child. Such a beautiful baby boy! As he grew he needed your special watchful care.

At his rebirth you are especially needed to keep him close to his Lord and filled with the Holy Spirit. Lead him to be a good father to his children. Guide him so that he knows true joy and happiness in his life. But, most importantly, lead him in his life so that he knows salvation and life eternal with his Father in Heaven.

My gratitude to you, John, for all of your loving care you've shown my son, Shawn.

Shawn's loving mother,
Judy

Dear Angel Ada,

Because of Shawn's special need you have recently been sent to him to be his second guardian angel. Thanks be to God in Heaven for granting this additional help. Please, along with John, lead my dear son on the paths of righteousness.

In the name of the Lord, thank you dear one.

Shawn's loving mother,
Judy

Dear Angel Caleb,

My baby, Micah Andrew, is in your special loving care. He was born on a sunny summer day, July 27th, 1975. Being almost one month early, he took a little extra special care after his birth. Micah was such a beautiful baby always smiling and happy.

Protect him from all the perils of life. Fill him with the joy of loving his Lord. See that he uses his talents to help in the Kingdom of God. Let Heaven with his Lord, Jesus Christ, be his eternal home.

Thank you, Caleb, for you are a very special angel.

Micah's loving mother,
Judy

Dear Angel Daniel,

You are the special guardian angel of my husband, and the love of my life, Arthur Thomas. He was born May 2, 1943, in Chicago, Illinois.

Arthur had a difficult childhood but you were there to care for him. You knew at his conception that he was chosen to greatness for his Lord. Humility, kindness, and compassion are only a few of his fine attributes. A finer husband and father cannot be found.

Daniel, you have been a visable and audible part of Arthur's life since the beginning of this year (1998). How very wonderful you are. Your guidance is filled with love and caring. Your humor is delightful! Words cannot express how much we love you and thank God for you.

May the time ahead be guided by your watchful eye and loving care. May the Lord's will be done in our lives and may Heaven be our home for all eternity.

Arthur's loving wife,

Judy

Dear Archangel Michael,

I am so filled with awe and wonder at your world of angels. Your interest in our lives, and visits to our home have made me feel so very humble.

I feel so totally unworthy of your heavenly realm. Knowing that you are so very close to our Lord fills my heart with joy.

Thank you, Archangel Michael, for writing the forward to this book. It's easy to see that you love mankind and want us to know the truth about the Lord's Word. I can only hope that the words in this book help to save many, many souls for the Lord.

Again, thank you, dear one, for all of your love and caring.

Yours in Christ,

Judy

BENEDICTION

Lord, dismiss us with Thy blessing,
Fill our hearts with joy and peace,
Let us each, Thy love possessing,
Triumph in redeeming grace.
Oh, refresh us, Oh, refresh us,
Trav'ling thro' this wilderness.

So whene'er the signal's given
Us from earth to call away,
Borne on angels' wings to heaven,
Glad the summons to obey,
May we ever, May we ever,
Reign with Christ in endless day!

By: John Fawcett (1773)

ABOUT THE AUTHOR

Dr. A. Thomas Smith is a practicing psychologist and educational consultant for a major city community school corporation in northern Indiana. His thirty plus years of experience within the field of education include nine years as a teacher and principal for Christian day schools. He has pulbished more that 250 articles concerning psychological and sociological aspects of family living. Dr. Smith is available for guest speaking engagements and seminar presentations on subjects including *Angels Among Us, Violence in the Schools and God's Plans to Prevent It, Teaching Family Values in Schools,* and *Assisting Disabled Students in the Classroom and at Home.* He may be contacted by letter at P.O. Box 654, Lakeside, MI 49116, by e-mail at asmith@sbcsc.k12.in.us, and by telephone at 616 469 0834.

Judy Strefling Smith is a homemaker and newspaper columnist. Her weekly column, *Homemakers,* published in the *Harbor Country News,* features recipes and information about food and its preparation for cooks who are just learning to cook and those who are quite accomplished. Her recipes focus on regional dishes, use of in-season fruits and vegetables, special holiday preparations, and international cuisines.